LANGUAGE!

The Comprehensive Literacy Curriculum

Bridge

Interactive Text
Book C

Reading
Writing
Spelling
Vocabulary
Grammar
Speaking

Jane Fell Greene, Ed.D.

Sopris West®

Sopris West®
EDUCATIONAL SERVICES

A Cambium Learning® Company

BOSTON, MA • LONGMONT, CO

12 11 10 09 08 8 7 6 5 4 3 2

Authors:
Jane Fell Greene, Ed.D.
Nancy Chapel Eberhardt

For acknowledgement of permissioned materials, see Sources, page R6.

ISBN 13 digit: 978-1-60218-745-0
ISBN 10 digit: 1-60218-745-2

Printed in the United States of America

Published and distributed by

Sopris West®
EDUCATIONAL SERVICES

A Cambium Learning® Company

4093 Specialty Place • Longmont, CO 80504 • (303) 651-2829
www.sopriswest.com

170510/9-08

Bridge

Table of Contents

Lesson Checklist 1-5

Check off the activities you complete with each lesson. Evaluate your accomplishments at the end of each lesson. Pay attention to teacher evaluations and comments.

	Unit Objectives	Lesson 1 (Date:_________)	Lesson 2 (Date:___________)
Phonemic Awareness and Phonics	❑ Segment sounds in words. ❑ Discriminate short sounds for vowels / ă /, / ĭ /, / ŏ /, / ĕ /, / ŭ /. ❑ Discriminate short and long vowel sounds. ❑ Segment syllables into words.	❑ Move It and Mark It ❑ Consonant Chart ❑ Vowel Chart	❑ Syllable Awareness: Segmentation
Word Recognition and Spelling	❑ Spell words and syllables containing short vowel sounds. ❑ Read and spell **Essential** (high-frequency) **Words** (U1–12). ❑ Spell words and syllables containing long vowel sounds represented by the final silent **e** pattern. ❑ Apply **Doubling Rule** for spelling. ❑ Apply **Drop e Rule** for spelling.		❑ Exercise 1: Listening for Word Parts
Vocabulary and Morphology	❑ Define words using categories and attributes. ❑ Identify the roles of inflectional endings.		❑ Define It
Grammar and Usage	❑ Identify nouns. ❑ Identify verbs. ❑ Identify adverbs and adverbial phrases. ❑ Identify adjectives and adjectival phrases. ❑ Identify verb tense.		❑ Exercise 2: Identify It: Nouns ❑ Exercise 3: Identify It: Verbs
Listening and Reading Comprehension	❑ Define vocabulary using context-based strategies. ❑ Read informational text to acquire and expand background knowledge.		
Speaking and Writing	❑ Generate sentences using a six-stage process. ❑ Use signal words to answer comprehension questions. ❑ Identify parts of a paragraph including a topic sentence, supporting detail sentences with transitions, elaborations, and a concluding sentence. ❑ Organize information to prepare to write. ❑ Write an expository paragraph.	❑ Masterpiece Sentences: Stages 1–6	❑ Masterpiece Sentences: Stage 1
	Self-Evaluation (5 is the highest) **Effort** = I produced my best work. **Participation** = I was actively involved in tasks. **Independence** = I worked on my own.	**Effort:** 1 2 3 4 5 **Participation:** 1 2 3 4 5 **Independence:** 1 2 3 4 5	**Effort:** 1 2 3 4 5 **Participation:** 1 2 3 4 5 **Independence:** 1 2 3 4 5
	Teacher Evaluation	**Effort:** 1 2 3 4 5 **Participation:** 1 2 3 4 5 **Independence:** 1 2 3 4 5	**Effort:** 1 2 3 4 5 **Participation:** 1 2 3 4 5 **Independence:** 1 2 3 4 5

Lesson 3 (Date:__________)	Lesson 4 (Date:__________)	Lesson 5 (Date:__________)
❑ Syllable Awareness: Segmentation ❑ Exercise 1: Listening for Word Parts	❑ Syllable Awareness: Segmentation	❑ Syllable Awareness: Segmentation
❑ Exercise 2: Pretest Essential Words	❑ Exercise 1: Listening for Word Parts ❑ Memorize It	❑ Exercise 1: Listening for Word Parts ❑ Memorize It
❑ Review: Verbs	❑ Review: Nouns	
❑ Masterpiece Sentences: Stages 2 and 3	❑ Masterpiece Sentences: Stage 4	❑ Masterpiece Sentences: Stage 5 ❑ Exercise 2: Check for Understanding: Lessons 1–5
Effort: 1 2 3 4 5 **Participation:** 1 2 3 4 5 **Independence:** 1 2 3 4 5	**Effort:** 1 2 3 4 5 **Participation:** 1 2 3 4 5 **Independence:** 1 2 3 4 5	**Effort:** 1 2 3 4 5 **Participation:** 1 2 3 4 5 **Independence:** 1 2 3 4 5
Effort: 1 2 3 4 5 **Participation:** 1 2 3 4 5 **Independence:** 1 2 3 4 5	**Effort:** 1 2 3 4 5 **Participation:** 1 2 3 4 5 **Independence:** 1 2 3 4 5	**Effort:** 1 2 3 4 5 **Participation:** 1 2 3 4 5 **Independence:** 1 2 3 4 5

Bridge • Lesson 2

Exercise 1 • Listening for Word Parts

- Listen to each word.
- Write the part your teacher repeats under the vowel sound you hear.

	Short a (/ ă /)	Short i (/ ĭ /)
1.		
2.		
3.		
4.		
5.		
6.		
7.		
8.		
9.		
10.		

Exercise 2 • Identify It: Nouns

- Read the selection with your teacher.
- Find the nouns–words that name people, places, things, and ideas.
- Underline the nouns.

based on "Bugs Live"

What is a bug? Bug is another word for insect. Scientists say that a bug's body has three segments. Bugs also have six legs. Look at a bee or a beetle. If you can spot three segments and six legs, you have spotted a bug.

Bugs live on people. They live on pets too. Bugs even live in pillows. You may make a wish that they aren't there. They are dust mites too small to see. They make our eyes red. They can make us sick. Bad bugs can gives us bad dreams.

- Sort the nouns into the correct columns.

People	Places	Things	Ideas

Bridge • Lesson 2

Exercise 3 • Identify It: Verbs

- Read each sentence.
- Identify and circle the verb—the word that answers: *What did they (he, she, it) do?*

1. Bugs eat crops.

2. We sweep the dust from the floor.

3. Insects love plants and pets.

4. Finding bugs is a big job.

5. Bugs chomp on plants' buds and stems.

6. Eggs hatch in the sod.

7. Our eyes get red from dust.

8. We fluff the blankets on our bed.

9. Some bugs help us.

10. He spots a dust mite.

- Sort the verbs into the correct columns.

Can see the action	Can't see the action

Exercise 1 • Listening for Word Parts

- Listen to each word.
- Write the part your teacher repeats under the vowel sound you hear.

	Short a (/ ă /)	Short i (/ ĭ /)	Short o (/ ŏ /)
1.			
2.			
3.			
4.			
5.			
6.			
7.			
8.			
9.			
10.			

Bridge • Lesson 3

Exercise 2 · Pretest: Essential Words (Book A)

▸ Write each word your teacher says.

Essential Words

1. ______________________
2. ______________________
3. ______________________
4. ______________________
5. ______________________
6. ______________________
7. ______________________
8. ______________________
9. ______________________
10. ______________________
11. ______________________
12. ______________________
13. ______________________
14. ______________________
15. ______________________
16. ______________________
17. ______________________
18. ______________________
19. ______________________
20. ______________________
21. ______________________
22. ______________________
23. ______________________
24. ______________________
25. ______________________
26. ______________________
27. ______________________
28. ______________________
29. ______________________
30. ______________________
31. ______________________
32. ______________________
33. ______________________
34. ______________________
35. ______________________
36. ______________________

Exercise 1 · Listening for Word Parts

- Listen to each word.
- Write the part your teacher repeats under the vowel sound you hear.

	Short i (/ ĭ /)	Short e (/ ĕ /)
1.		
2.		
3.		
4.		
5.		
6.		
7.		
8.		
9.		
10.		

Bridge • Lesson 4

Exercise 2 • Identify It: Nouns

- Read each sentence.
- Underline all nouns.
- Identify the subject and circle it. Remember to ask: *Who (what) did it?* to help determine which noun is the subject of the sentence.

1. During the early morning, the class watched the family of ducks with green feathers on the pond.
2. The labs tugged at the rug and broke the lamp.
3. The students hunted for the chinch bugs in the grass.
4. At sunset, Kim played his drums in the park.
5. Puffins pick fish from the ocean.
6. Sitting in the warm sun, Ali ate the cold plums.
7. Bud had scratches on his legs from the thorny bushes.
8. Jill's mom picked up two bags of shrimp for the picnic.
9. Mr. Morey's class pushed their desks across the room.
10. The spider spun a silken web between the trees.

Exercise 1 • Listening for Word Parts

- Listen to each word.
- Write the part your teacher repeats under the vowel sound you hear.

	Short a (/ ă /)	Short i (/ ĭ /)	Short o (/ ŏ /)	Short e (/ ĕ /)	Short u (/ ŭ /)	Short u (/ o͝o /)
1.						
2.						
3.						
4.						
5.						
6.						
7.						
8.						
9.						
10.						

Bridge • Lesson 5

Exercise 2 • Check for Understanding: Lessons 1–5

- Read the selection.
- Use the Handbook section of the *Student Text* if needed.

based on "New Old Insects"

Oliver Zompro is a scientist. He looks for old insects. How? People send him chunks of amber. Amber is hard as rock. Zompro finds old insects in the amber. Amber was a sticky gum long ago. It dripped from trees and covered the insects. Amber trapped them inside. Zompro thinks about these insects. He has an idea. Do insects like them still live? Other scientists go to Africa. They hunt for such insects in the bush. They find new insects. They put new insects next to the old insects caught in the amber. They smile. They are the same.

- Find two examples of each short vowel sounds in the selection. Choose **one-syllable words**. Write the words in the correct column.

<u>a</u> (/ ă /)	<u>e</u> (/ ĕ /)	<u>i</u> (/ ĭ /)	<u>o</u> (/ ŏ /)	<u>u</u> (/ ŭ /)

- Find two examples of **<u>u</u>** for the sound / o͞o /. Write them on the line.

____

(continued)

Exercise 2 • Check for Understanding: Lessons 1–5 *(continued)*

▸ Find examples for each category of nouns in the selection. Write the nouns in the correct column.

Person	Place	Thing	Idea

▸ Find examples of verbs in the selection. Write the verbs in the correct columns.

Actions you can see	Actions you can't see

▸ Select a noun and verb from the charts above to write a base sentence. Then, use information from the selection to complete the remaining stages of the **Masterpiece Six-Stage Process**. Write your sentence here.

Lesson Checklist 6–10

Check off the activities you complete with each lesson. Evaluate your accomplishments at the end of each lesson. Pay attention to teacher evaluations and comments.

	Unit Objectives	**Lesson 6** (Date:________)	**Lesson 7** (Date:__________)
Phonemic Awareness and Phonics	❑ Segment sounds in words. ❑ Discriminate short sounds for vowels / ă /, / ĭ /, / ŏ /, / ĕ /, / ŭ /. ❑ Discriminate short and long vowel sounds. ❑ Segment syllables into words.	❑ Move It and Mark It ❑ Vowel + Consonant + e Pattern ❑ Vowel Chart	❑ Listening for Sounds in Words ❑ Vowel + Consonant + e Pattern
Word Recognition and Spelling	❑ Spell words and syllables containing short vowel sounds. ❑ Read and spell **Essential** (high-frequency) **Words** (U1–12). ❑ Spell words and syllables containing long vowel sounds represented by the final silent **e** pattern. ❑ Apply **Doubling Rule** for spelling. ❑ Apply **Drop e Rule** for spelling.		
Vocabulary and Morphology	❑ Define words using categories and attributes. ❑ Identify the roles of inflectional endings.		
Grammar and Usage	❑ Identify nouns. ❑ Identify verbs. ❑ Identify adverbs and adverbial phrases. ❑ Identify adjectives and adjectival phrases. ❑ Identify verb tense.		❑ Review: Masterpiece Sentences ❑ Exercise 1: Diagram It 1
Listening and Reading Comprehension	❑ Define vocabulary using context-based strategies. ❑ Read informational text to acquire and expand background knowledge.	❑ Read the Selection: **"Telling Time"**	❑ Read the Selection: **"Time Zones"**
Speaking and Writing	❑ Generate sentences using a six-stage process. ❑ Use signal words to answer comprehension questions. ❑ Identify parts of a paragraph including a topic sentence, supporting detail sentences with transitions, elaborations, and a concluding sentence. ❑ Organize information to prepare to write. ❑ Write an expository paragraph.	❑ Exercise 1: Answer It: Using Signal Words	❑ Exercise 2: Answer It: Using Signal Words
	Self-Evaluation (5 is the highest) **Effort** = I produced my best work. **Participation** = I was actively involved in tasks. **Independence** = I worked on my own.	**Effort:** 1 2 3 4 5 **Participation:** 1 2 3 4 5 **Independence:** 1 2 3 4 5	**Effort:** 1 2 3 4 5 **Participation:** 1 2 3 4 5 **Independence:** 1 2 3 4 5
	Teacher Evaluation	**Effort:** 1 2 3 4 5 **Participation:** 1 2 3 4 5 **Independence:** 1 2 3 4 5	**Effort:** 1 2 3 4 5 **Participation:** 1 2 3 4 5 **Independence:** 1 2 3 4 5

Lesson 8 (Date:____________)	Lesson 9 (Date:____________)	Lesson 10 (Date:____________)
❏ Exercise 1: Listening for Word Parts ❏ Exercise 2: Pretest Essential Words	❏ Exercise 1: Listening for Word Parts ❏ Memorize It	❏ Exercise 1: Listening for Word Parts ❏ Memorize It
❏ Review: Masterpiece Sentences: Stage 2 Diagram It	❏ Diagram It: Predicate Painters and Subject Painters	
❏ Paragraph Structure	❏ Exercise 2: Number Topic Sentences	❏ Exercise 2: Write It: Topic Sentences ❏ Exercise 3: Organizing Information ❏ Exercise 4: Check for Understanding: Lessons 6–10
Effort: 1 2 3 4 5 **Participation:** 1 2 3 4 5 **Independence:** 1 2 3 4 5	**Effort:** 1 2 3 4 5 **Participation:** 1 2 3 4 5 **Independence:** 1 2 3 4 5	**Effort:** 1 2 3 4 5 **Participation:** 1 2 3 4 5 **Independence:** 1 2 3 4 5
Effort: 1 2 3 4 5 **Participation:** 1 2 3 4 5 **Independence:** 1 2 3 4 5	**Effort:** 1 2 3 4 5 **Participation:** 1 2 3 4 5 **Independence:** 1 2 3 4 5	**Effort:** 1 2 3 4 5 **Participation:** 1 2 3 4 5 **Independence:** 1 2 3 4 5

TELLING TIME

Throughout history, people have had different ways of telling time. Ancient people used the sun or water to tell time. Later on, they used candles. Then, people made clocks with weights and springs. Nowadays, people use atomic particles to measure time very exactly.

One of the first time-telling devices was the sundial. It was used in ancient Egypt as early as 3500 BC. The sundial told the hour of the day by measuring the sun's shadow. The sun almost always shines in Egypt, so the sundial was a good **method** for the early Egyptians to use.

method
a way of doing something

Around 400 BC, the ancient Greeks started using water to tell time. Their water clock consisted of a **vessel** containing water. Markings on the inside of the vessel measured the outflow of water. It also measured the passing of the hours.

vessel
a hollow object used for holding liquids or objects

Later on, people burned candles to tell time. Around the year 1000 AD, two different civilizations got the idea to tell time this way. These two civilizations were far away from each other, but they each came up with the same time-telling method. Alfred the Great was a Saxon king. He ruled in an area that is now part of England. The Saxons burned candles to tell time. The Sung Dynasty ruled in China at about the same period. They too burned candles to mark time.

During the 1400s, the first mechanical clocks appeared in Europe. They used a mainspring and balance wheel. Then, telling time relied on a mechanical device.

Finally, around 1950, we began to use atomic clocks. Isidor Rabi, a **physicist**, first thought of this idea. His clock was based on the study of **atoms**. Atomic clocks measure the vibrations of atoms. By 1967, the way we tell time became even more **precise**. One second was defined as 9,192,631,770 vibrations of the cesium atom. In 1999, the latest atomic clock came online. It had even more incredible accuracy. Now everyone around the world measures time the same way. Telling time does not **vary** anymore.

physicist
a scientist who studies matter, energy, motion, and force

atoms
the smallest parts of an element

precise
exact

vary
to change or become different from something else

Answer It

Answer each question in one or more complete sentences.

1. When did the Egyptians use the sundial to tell time?
2. Identify four other methods people have used to tell time.
3. Explain how the Greeks used water to measure time.
4. Identify two parts of a mechanical clock.
5. Explain how people started telling time with atomic clocks.

Bridge • Lesson 6

Exercise 1 · Answer It: Using Signal Words

- Underline the signal word and answer each question.
- Then underline the part of the answer that replaces the signal word.

1. When did the Egyptians use the sundial to tell time?

____

____

2. Identify four other methods people have used to tell time.

____

____

3. Explain how the Greeks used water to measure time.

____

____

4. Identify two parts of a mechanical clock.

____

____

5. Explain how people started telling time with atomic clocks.

____

____

Exercise 1 • Diagram It 1

- Look at the picture your teacher displays.
- Fill in the diagram to answer the questions based on the picture.
- Use the diagram to say a complete sentence.

1.

Who (what) did it?	What did they (he, she, it) do?
Cat	**walked**

2.

Who (what) did it?	What did they (he, she, it) do?

3.

Who (what) did it?	What did they (he, she, it) do?

4.

Who (what) did it?	What did they (he, she, it) do?

5.

Who (what) did it?	What did they (he, she, it) do?

Bridge • Lesson 7

Time Zones

The map is divided into shapes that show the different time zones. The line divides day and night.

zones
areas that are different from others because of certain features or characteristics

divided
separated into sections or parts

local
nearby; in the same, specific area

imaginary
not real

Is it day where you live? If so, it is night on the opposite side of planet Earth. It could also be today or tomorrow, depending on where you are. If this is confusing, don't worry. There is an explanation, and it has to do with time **zones**.

The Earth is **divided** into different time zones, with one time zone for each hour of the day. Since there are 24 hours in a day, that means there are 24 different time zones. **Local** times are different all over the world. How did we ever figure it all out? Scientists and others had to develop a worldwide time zone system.

First, they had to decide how to divide up the Earth. They decided to use longitude, which is a system of **imaginary** lines. These lines don't really exist, but they are shown on globes and maps. They are vertical and pass through the North and South poles. New time zones begin at about every 15 degrees longitude. You can see them on the map on the previous page.

Then, scientists needed to decide where time zones would begin. Which longitude line would be the starting point? They chose a **random** longitude line, which they called the *prime meridian*. This longitude line passes through Greenwich, England, marked with an x on the map on the previous page. It is labeled "zero degrees longitude." Greenwich Mean Time (GMT) **refers** to the time in Greenwich, England. This is the longitudinal starting point for all time zones. GMT is also called Universal Time (UT) or Zulu time (Z).

random
without a plan or pattern

refers
relates to; means

Finally, a 24-hour clock had to be created. Our 12-hour clocks were confusing. People would confuse 3:00 a.m. with 3:00 p.m.! On a 24-hour clock, midnight is 0:00 and noon is 12:00, so 2:00 p.m. is 14:00. See if you can figure this out. What number would be used for 8:00 p.m. on the 24-hour clock? (If you answered 20:00, you're right!)

Now, find the time zone where you live. What time is it? Count 12 time zones to the east. That is to the right. You are looking at the opposite side of the Earth from where you live. If it is day where you are, it is night there!

Answer It

Answer each question in one or more complete sentences.

1. Identify the number of time zones scientists created.
2. Discuss why longitude is important in telling time.
3. Paraphrase how scientists decided where time zones would begin by replacing the underlined words in the sentence below with your own words.

   <u>Scientists chose</u> a random <u>longitude line</u>.
4. Explain what GMT is.
5. Discuss why a 24-hour clock was needed.

On the 24-hour clock, midnight is 0:00. Noon is 12:00, so 2:00 p.m. is 14:00.

Bridge • Lesson 7

Exercise 2 · Answer It: Using Signal Words

- Underline the signal word and answer each question.
- Then underline the part of the answer that replaces the signal word.

1. Identify the number of time zones scientists created.

2. Discuss why longitude is important in telling time.

3. Paraphrase how scientists decided where time zones would begin by replacing the underlined words in the sentence below with your own words.

   Scientists chose a random longitude line.

4. Explain what GMT is.

5. Discuss why a 24-hour clock was needed.

Exercise 1 • Listening for Word Parts

▶ Listen to each word.

▶ Write the part your teacher repeats under the vowel sound you hear.

	Long a (/ ā /)	Long e (/ ē /)	Long i (/ ī /)	Long o (/ ō /)	Long u (/ o͞o /) or	(/ yo͞o /)
1.						
2.						
3.						
4.						
5.						
6.						
7.						
8.						
9.						
10.						

Exercise 2 • Pretest: Essential Words (Book B)

▸ Write each word your teacher says.

Essential Words

1. ______________________
2. ______________________
3. ______________________
4. ______________________
5. ______________________
6. ______________________
7. ______________________
8. ______________________
9. ______________________
10. ______________________
11. ______________________
12. ______________________
13. ______________________
14. ______________________
15. ______________________
16. ______________________
17. ______________________
18. ______________________
19. ______________________
20. ______________________
21. ______________________
22. ______________________
23. ______________________
24. ______________________
25. ______________________
26. ______________________
27. ______________________
28. ______________________
29. ______________________
30. ______________________
31. ______________________
32. ______________________
33. ______________________
34. ______________________
35. ______________________
36. ______________________

Exercise 3 • Parts of a Paragraph

- Read the paragraph.
- Highlight:
  - the **topic sentence** in green.
  - the **supporting details plus transitions** in yellow.
  - circle the **transition** words
  - **explanations** in red or pink.
  - the **conclusion** in green.
- Then write a label next to each part of the paragraph.

1. ______________________________

   ____

2. ______________________________

   ____

3. ______________________________

   ____

4. ______________________________

   ____

5. ______________________________

   ____

6. ______________________________

   ____

The Benefits of Exercise

Regular exercise benefits people's health in two important ways. One benefit is that exercise improves people's physical health. It makes the heart, lungs, bones, and muscles stronger and keeps people at a healthy weight. Exercise is also good for the mind. It makes people feel better about themselves, and calms them down when they are angry or stressed. When people regularly do physical activities they enjoy, their bodies and minds stay fit, happy, and healthy.

Exercise 1 • Listening for Word Parts

- Listen to each word.
- Write the part your teacher repeats under the vowel sound you hear.

	Long a (/ā/)	Long e (/ē/)	Long i (/ī/)	Long o (/ō/)	Long u (/o͞o/) or	(/yo͞o/)
1.						
2.						
3.						
4.						
5.						
6.						
7.						
8.						
9.						
10.						

Exercise 2 · Number Topic Sentences

- Read each topic sentence.
- Underline the words that tell the topic. Circle any number words.
- Then answer the questions.

1. Three cities have serious pollution problems.

What is the topic?____________________________________

What will the writer need to tell about the topic?__________________

____

2. Maps have multiple layers of information.

What is the topic?____________________________________

What will the writer need to tell about the topic?__________________

____

3. In winter, I watch two high school sports.

What is the topic?____________________________________

What will the writer need to tell about the topic?__________________

____

4. I enjoy several kinds of music.

What is the topic?____________________________________

What will the writer need to tell about the topic? __________________

____

5. At our school, the band raises money in three ways.

What is the topic?____________________________________

What will the writer need to tell about the topic?__________________

____

Bridge • Lesson 10

Exercise 1 • Listening for Word Parts

- Listen to each word.
- Write the part your teacher repeats in the correct column.

	Short vowel sound	Long vowel sound
1.		
2.		
3.		
4.		
5.		
6.		
7.		
8.		
9.		
10.		

Exercise 2 • Write It: Number Topic Sentences

▸ Read the topic and the supporting details.

▸ Then use them to write a Number Topic Sentence.

1. Topic: bugs cause problems
   Supporting Details:
   transmit illnesses
   damage crops
   Topic Sentence:____

2. Topic: ways to tell time
   Supporting Details:
   sundial
   burning candles
   mechanical clocks
   Topic Sentence:____

3. Topic: favorite foods
   Supporting Details:
   pizza
   fruit salad
   Topic Sentence:____

4. Topic: swimming safety
   Supporting Details:
   know your own abilities
   walk around the pool
   don't dive
   Topic Sentence:____

5. Topic: qualities of your best friend
   Supporting Details:
   good listener
   shares things with you
   makes you laugh
   Topic Sentence:____

Bridge • Lesson 10

Exercise 3: Organizing Information

- Select one of the topics from Exercise 2, **Write It: Number Topic Sentences**, on page 29.
- Use that topic and the supporting details that are provided to fill in the **Blueprint for Writing**.
- Add elaborations for the supporting details based on your knowledge and experience.

Blueprint for Writing

Informal (Two-Column) Outline

- Use the information on the **Blueprint for Writing** to create an **Informal (Two-Column) Outline.**

Topic:

☆	
☆	
☆	

Excercise 4: Check for Understanding: Lessons 6–10

- Read the selection and follow the directions below.
- Use the Handbook section of the *Student Text* as needed.

based on "Telling Time"

Throughout history, people have had different ways of telling time. One of the first ways people used to tell time was the sundial. It was used in ancient Egypt about 3500 BC. The sundial told the hour of the day by measuring the sun's shadow. Around 400 BC, the Greeks started using water to tell time. They marked the inside of a vessel and measured the outflow of water. The markings also marked the passing of the hours. Around 1000 AD, people in Europe and China used candles to tell time. During the 1400s, the first mechanical clocks were made in Europe. They used a mainspring and a balance wheel to measure the passage of time. Around 1950, we began using atomic clocks. Isidor Rabi, a physicist, first had the idea. Atomic clocks measure the vibrations of atoms. Throughout history, people have been interested in creating more precise ways to tell time.

- Find three examples of words with the long vowel sound using the final silent <u>e</u> pattern. Write the words here.

____

- Reread the paragraph in the box. Underline the topic sentence. Circle the words that tell the topic.
- Answer the following question using the Answer It process.

Identify the different ways that people have told time through history.

____

____

Check off the activities you complete with each lesson. Evaluate your accomplishments at the end of each lesson. Pay attention to teacher evaluations and comments.

	Unit Objectives	Lesson 11 (Date:________)	Lesson 12 (Date:________)
Phonemic Awareness and Phonics	❑ Segment sounds in words. ❑ Discriminate short sounds for vowels / ă /, / ĭ /, / ŏ /, / ĕ /, / ŭ /. ❑ Discriminate short and long vowel sounds. ❑ Segment syllables into words.	❑ Exercise 1: Syllable Segmentation	❑ Exercise 1: Syllable Segmentation
Word Recognition and Spelling	❑ Spell words and syllables containing short vowel sounds. ❑ Read and spell **Essential** (high-frequency) **Words** (U1–12) ❑ Spell words and syllables containing long vowel sounds represented by final silent **e** pattern. ❑ Apply **Doubling Rule** for spelling. ❑ Apply **Drop e Rule** for spelling.	❑ Memorize It	❑ Memorize It
Vocabulary and Morphology	❑ Define words using categories and attributes. ❑ Identify the roles of inflectional endings.		
Grammar and Usage	❑ Identify nouns. ❑ Identify verbs. ❑ Identify adverbs and adverbial phrases. ❑ Identify adjectives and adjectival phrases. ❑ Identify verb tense.		
Listening and Reading Comprehension	❑ Define vocabulary using context-based strategies. ❑ Read informational text to acquire and expand background knowledge.	❑ Exercise 2: Use the Clues: Vocabulary Strategies	❑ Exercise 2: Use the Clues Vocabulary Strategies
Speaking and Writing	❑ Generate sentences using a six-stage process. ❑ Use signal words to answer comprehension questions. ❑ Identify parts of a paragraph including a topic sentence, supporting detail sentences with transitions, elaborations, and a concluding sentence. ❑ Organize information to prepare to write. ❑ Write an expository paragraph.	❑ Exercise 3: Supporting Detail Sentences ❑ Exercise 4: Transitional Words and Phrases	❑ Exercise 3: Elaborations: Examples, Explanations, and Evidence
	Self-Evaluation (5 is the highest) **Effort** = I produced my best work. **Participation** = I was actively involved in tasks. **Independence** = I worked on my own.	**Effort:** 1 2 3 4 5 **Participation:** 1 2 3 4 5 **Independence:** 1 2 3 4 5	**Effort:** 1 2 3 4 5 **Participation:** 1 2 3 4 5 **Independence:** 1 2 3 4 5
	Teacher Evaluation	**Effort:** 1 2 3 4 5 **Participation:** 1 2 3 4 5 **Independence:** 1 2 3 4 5	**Effort:** 1 2 3 4 5 **Participation:** 1 2 3 4 5 **Independence:** 1 2 3 4 5

Lesson 13 (Date:__________)	Lesson 14 (Date:__________)	Lesson 15 (Date:__________)
	❏ The **Doubling Rule** for Spelling ❏ Double It	❏ **The Drop e Rule** for Spelling ❏ Drop It
❏ Exercise 1: Identify It: Inflectional Suffixes		
❏ Tense Timeline		
❏ Exercise 2: Use the Clues Vocabulary Strategies	❏ Exercise 1: Use the Clues Vocabulary Strategies ❏ Read the Selection: **"Hurricane!"**	
❏ Exercise 3: Informal (Two-Column) Outline	❏ Prepare to Write an Expository Paragraph	❏ Write It: Expository Paragraph ❏ Exercise 1: Check for Understanding: Lessons 11–15
Effort: 1 2 3 4 5 **Participation:** 1 2 3 4 5 **Independence:** 1 2 3 4 5	**Effort:** 1 2 3 4 5 **Participation:** 1 2 3 4 5 **Independence:** 1 2 3 4 5	**Effort:** 1 2 3 4 5 **Participation:** 1 2 3 4 5 **Independence:** 1 2 3 4 5
Effort: 1 2 3 4 5 **Participation:** 1 2 3 4 5 **Independence:** 1 2 3 4 5	**Effort:** 1 2 3 4 5 **Participation:** 1 2 3 4 5 **Independence:** 1 2 3 4 5	**Effort:** 1 2 3 4 5 **Participation:** 1 2 3 4 5 **Independence:** 1 2 3 4 5

Bridge • Lesson 11

Exercise 1 • Syllable Segmentation

- Listen to the word your teacher says.
- Repeat the word.
- Count the syllables in the word.
- Write the letter for each vowel sound you hear. Use a diacritical mark to show if the sound is short (˘) or long (¯).

	How many syllables do you hear?	First vowel sound	Second vowel sound	Third vowel sound
1.				
2.				
3.				
4.				
5.				
6.				
7.				
8.				
9.				
10.				

Exercise 2 • Use the Clues: Vocabulary Strategies

1. Work along with your teacher to define the term **prime meridian**.

The longitude line that is the start point for time zones is called the prime meridian. It passes through Greenwich, England. It is labeled "zero degrees longitude."

2. Use meaning cues to define **longitude**.

- Underline the term.
- Read the sentence aloud and look for a meaning cue.
- Circle the meaning cue.
- Double underline the words that define **longitude**.
- Draw an arrow from the word **longitude** to the definition.

based on "Time Zones"

First, they had to decide how to divide up the Earth. They decided to use longitude, which is a system of imaginary lines. These lines don't really exist, but they are shown on globes and maps. They are vertical and pass through the North and South poles. New time zones begin at about every 15 degrees longitude.

3. Define the word **longitude** in your own words.

____

____

____

4. Verify your definition of the word **longitude** by using a dictionary reference source.

5. How did scientists use **longitude**?

____

____

Exercise 3 · Supporting Detail Sentences

- Listen to your teacher read each **topic sentence** and the possible supporting detail sentences below it.
- Identify and check two sentences that are **supporting details** for that topic sentence.
- Then write a third supporting detail sentence of your own.

1. **Topic Sentence:**
   Breakfast is an important meal for several reasons.

   Possible Supporting Detail Sentences:
   _______ My favorite breakfast is cereal with bananas.
   _______ Dinner is also a very important meal.
   _______ Most people wake up hungry in the morning.
   _______ People's bodies have been working overnight as they were sleeping.

   _______ ____

2. **Topic Sentence:**
   Team sports teach kids several helpful lessons.

   Possible Supporting Detail Sentences:
   _______ Kids learn about working together.
   _______ Baseball and soccer are team sports.
   _______ My favorite team sport is football.
   _______ Kids learn that playing is about having fun, not just winning.

   _______ ____

3. **Topic Sentence:**
   Smoking causes a number of problems.

   Possible Supporting Detail Sentences:
   _______ I don't like the smell of smoke.
   _______ Smoking pollutes the air for others to breathe.
   _______ Smoking can be a fire hazard.
   _______ People cannot smoke in most restaurants.

   _______ ____

(continued)

Exercise 3 • Supporting Detail Sentences *(continued)*

4. **Topic Sentence:**
During cold and flu season, people should do three things to stay healthy.

Possible Supporting Detail Sentences:
_______ They should wash their hands often.
_______ In the summer, people don't get colds as much.
_______ When people have colds, they cough and sneeze.
_______ They should drink juice and eat foods rich in vitamin C.

_______ ____

5. **Topic Sentence:**
Dogs are wonderful pets in several ways.

Possible Supporting Detail Sentences:
_______ You can take dogs running with you.
_______ Dogs are very loyal.
_______ Cats are also wonderful animals.
_______ The best dogs are beagles.

_______ ____

Bridge • Lesson 11

Exercise 4 • Transitional Words and Phrases

- Read the transitional words in the box.
- Then, read each topic sentence.
- Choose transition words from the box and write them at the beginning of the supporting detail sentences.

First	Second	Third	Finally	Another
One	Next	Then	Also	Last

1. Breakfast is an important meal for several reasons.

___________, most people wake up hungry in the morning.

___________, people's bodies have been working overnight as they were sleeping.

___________, breakfast gives people energy to get through the day.

2. Team sports teach kids several helpful lessons.

___________ reason is that kids learn about working together.

___________ reason is that kids learn that playing is about having fun, not just winning.

A__________ reason is that kids discover that they can learn new skills from teammates.

3. Smoking causes a number of problems.

___________, smoking pollutes the air for others to breathe.

___________, smoking can be a fire hazard.

___________, smoking causes illnesses.

(continued)

Exercise 4 • Transitional Words and Phrases *(continued)*

4. During cold and flu season, people should do three things to stay healthy.

______________, they should wash their hands often.

______________, they should drink juice and eat foods rich in vitamin C.

______________, they should get lots of sleep.

5. Dogs are wonderful pets in several ways.

______________ way they are wonderful pets is that you can take dogs running with you.

______________ way is that dogs are loyal.

A______________ way is that dogs protect you.

Bridge • Lesson 12

Exercise 1 • Syllable Segmentation

- Listen to the word your teacher says.
- Repeat the word.
- Count the syllables in the word.
- Write the letter for each vowel sound you hear. Use a diacritical mark to show if the sound is short (˘) or long (¯).

	How many syllables do you hear?	First vowel sound	Second vowel sound	Third vowel sound
1.				
2.				
3.				
4.				
5.				
6.				
7.				
8.				
9.				
10.				

Exercise 2 • Use the Clues: Vocabulary Strategies

1. Use meaning cues along with your teacher to define **eye**.

The center of a storm is called the eye.

2. Use meaning cues to define **Coriolis effect**.
   - Underline the term.
   - Read the sentence aloud and look for a meaning cue.
   - Circle the meaning cue.
   - Double underline the words that define **Coriolis effect**.
   - Draw an arrow from the word **Coriolis effect** to the definition

from "Hurricanes!"

Hurricanes are not like ordinary storms. They are different. They have powerful spinning winds. The winds rotate. They whip around the storm center. The center of the storm is called the eye. Earth's rotation affects the direction of the spin. North of the equator, winds spin to the right. In the south, they spin to the left. This is called the *Coriolis effect*. These whirling winds are dangerous. They cause a thunderstorm to form. It will become a tropical storm. Then it will become a hurricane.

3. Define the term **Coriolis effect** in your own words.

____

____

____

____

4. Verify your definition of the term **Coriolis effec**t by using a dictionary reference source.

Exercise 3 · Elaborations: Examples, Explanations, and Evidence

The sentences in the box are part of a paragraph. Listen to your teacher read those sentences and the list of possible Elaborations, or E's, to you.

Select E's from the list to make the supporting details clearer. Write your selection on the line.

Possible E's

For example, it causes lung cancer.
Smoke that affects other people is called secondhand smoke.
Smoking caused three of the worst wildfires in California between 1929 and 1999.
Secondhand smoke can harm the health of those around the person smoking.
It is also a major cause of heart disease.
Smoking is the leading cause of fire deaths.

Smoking causes a number of problems. First, smoking pollutes the air that others breathe. ______________________________

____

____

Second, smoking can be a fire hazard. ______________________________

____

____

Third, smoking causes illnesses. ______________________________

____

____

Exercise 1 • Identify It: Inflectional Suffixes

- Read each sentence and underline the word with an inflectional suffix.
- Think about the way the underlined word functions in the sentence.
  Ask:
  Does it make the word mean more than one?
  Does it make the word show possession?
  Does it make the word show the tense (time)?
- Place a check mark in the column to indicate the meaning of the suffix.
- Refer to the Handbook section of the *Student Text*, page H25, for the list of inflectional suffixes as needed.

		Number (more than one)	Possession	Tense (time)
1.	Kites have many shapes and uses.			
2.	The price of the stocks fell.			
3.	He stocks the pond with fish each spring.			
4.	He is flying a kite.			
5.	The kite's tail is long.			
6.	Hargrave invented the box kite.			
7.	The student's desk was clean.			
8.	This tool has many practical uses.			
9.	Winds spin around the eye of the storm.			
10.	He took the enemy's palace.			

Bridge · Lesson 13

Exercise 2 · Use the Clues: Vocabulary Strategies

1. Use substitutions along with your teacher to define **muffeleta.**

What was the grandfather of the sub? It was probably the muffuletta. People in New Orleans still love this traditional multi-layered sandwich.

2. Use substitutions to define the word **condiments**.

- Underline the word **condiments**.
- Read the text surrounding the word, looking for substitution clues.
- Double underline the words that define **condiments**.
- Draw an arrow from the unfamiliar word to its definition.

from "Making Hero Sandwiches"

First, hold a loaf of French bread on its side. Second, slice the bread in half lengthwise. Next, layer on slices of meat and cheese. Ham and salami can be used. Provolone, Swiss, or American cheese can be used. Then, top with lettuce and tomato. After that, add onions, pickles, olives, and hot peppers. Hot peppers and onions are optional. Finally, spread on mayonnaise or mustard. Other condiments can be added, too. A drizzle of Italian salad dressing adds a little spice.

3. Define the word **condiments** in your own words.

____

____

____

4. Verify your definition of the word **condiments** by using a dictionary reference source.

Exercise 3 • Informal (Two-Column) Outline

- Review the **Informal (Two-Column) Outline** below.
- Highlight the topic in green.
- Highlight the supporting details (stars) in yellow.
- Highlight the elaborations (dashes) in red.

Topic: the benefits of regular exercise

☆ improves people's physical health	—makes heart, lungs, bones, and muscles stronger —keeps people at healthy weight
☆ good for the mind	—makes people feel better about themselves —calms people down when angry or stressed

- Turn to the Handbook section of the *Student Text*, page H88.
- Read each sentence of the paragraph **"The Benefits of Exercise."**
- Look at the relationship of the outline to the paragraph.

Bridge • Lesson 14

Exercise 1 • Use the Clues: Vocabulary Strategies

1. Work along with your teacher to use pronoun referents to define the word **amber**.

Amber is full of very old insects. It is a gum from trees that covers the insects and then becomes hard as stone.

2. Use pronoun referents to define the word **entomologist**.

- Underline the unfamiliar word.
- Read the text surrounding the unfamiliar word, looking for a pronoun that takes the place of the unfamiliar word (noun).
- Circle the pronoun.
- Draw an arrow from the pronoun to the noun it replaces.
- Double underline the words that help define the unfamiliar word (noun).
- Draw an arrow from the pronoun to the words that help define the unfamiliar word.

adapted from "New Old Insects"

Oliver Zompro is an entomologist. He is a scientist who studies insects. He comes from Germany. Zompro loves insects. People send him chunks of amber. Why do they send him amber? Why does Zompro want to study it? Amber is a rare stone that is full of ancient insects.

3. Define **entomologist** in your own words:

____

____

4. Verify your definition of the term **entomologist by** using a dictionary reference source.

5. Name an entomologist.

____

It's summer, and hurricane season is coming! Hurricanes are strong and dangerous storms that twist and spin and take unpredictable paths. They are also very big, some covering an area hundreds of miles wide. These storms are feared because their powerful winds and heavy rains threaten life and **property**.

property
things or land that belong to someone

Hurricanes begin in the late summer in tropical seas where the water is warm. How warm does the water have to be? The answer is, very warm. The surface of the sea must be at least 80 degrees Fahrenheit, or 26 degrees Centigrade.

ordinary
common; plain; not special

Hurricanes are not like **ordinary** storms. They have powerful, spinning winds that whip around the storm's center, or eye. The rotation of the Earth affects the direction in which the winds spin around the eye. North of the equator, winds spin to the right, while in the south, they spin to the left. This is called the *Coriolis effect*. These whirling winds are very dangerous. They can form into a powerful thunderstorm, which can become a tropical storm and eventually turn into a hurricane.

To begin, strong thunderstorms form over open seas. This happens in warm Atlantic water during the late summer. Warm, wet air rises from the sea, condenses, and turns into clouds. Then, the heat and moisture come together. The heat "bursts," and several strong thunderstorms combine. Can you guess what will happen if they keep growing? They will eventually become a powerful hurricane.

band
a group of things or people moving or working together

The thunderstorms form where there is a **band** of low pressure. They combine together and create a thunderstorm cluster. This cluster becomes an organized system with a **definite** area. Its winds are strong and fast, with speeds between 39 and 73 miles per hour. The winds spin around and around, and a tropical storm is born.

definite
exact; specific; clearly defined

For the tropical storm to become a hurricane, two things must be in place. They are wind strength and wind spin. First, the sustained winds must be at least 74 miles per hour. A sustained wind is a **continuous** wind. Many storms have strong wind gusts, but sustained winds are not gusting winds or short winds. Second, the winds spin around the eye of the storm. When these two events happen, the storm can become a hurricane!

continuous
going without stopping

The hurricane builds strength by feeding on warm, moist air. It begins to move, traveling at speeds between 10 and 50 miles per hour.

Spanish explorers, **en route** to the West Indies after Columbus, encountered storms of incredible violence. Called *huracan*, or "evil wind," by the local people, these storms are now known as hurricanes.

en route
on the way

The towering clouds form a wind wall. This wall, surrounding the eye of the storm, holds the strongest winds and the heaviest rains. The strong winds spin wildly, whirling around the eye. Their speeds are intense, sometimes approaching 200 miles per hour. If the hurricane hits land, flooding and destruction will follow.

Eventually, the hurricane enters a cold, unfriendly surrounding and dies down. When it hits an area of cool land or water, it loses its supply of hot, moist air, and there is nothing to feed it. The winds weaken, the eye disappears, and the storm is dead.

How are hurricanes categorized?

The hurricane scale is numbered one to five. Categories are based on wind strength. The categories are described in the chart below.

HURRICANE INTENSITY CHART

The Hurricane Scale ranks hurricanes from **Category 1** to **Category 5.**

- **Category 1 Hurricane**. Winds 74-95 mph (64-82 kt). No real damage to buildings. Damage to mobile homes. Some damage to poorly built signs. Also, some coastal flooding. Minor pier damage.
- **Category 2 Hurricane**. Winds 96-110 mph (83-95 kt). Some damage to building roofs, doors, and windows. Considerable damage to mobile homes. Flooding damages piers. Small craft in unprotected moorings may break their moorings. Some trees blown down.
- **Category 3 Hurricane**. Winds 111-130 mph (96-113 kt). Some structural damage to small residences and utility buildings. Large trees blown down. Mobile homes and poorly built signs destroyed. Flooding near the coast destroys small structures. Large structures damaged by floating debris. Land may flood far inland.
- **Category 4 Hurricane**. Winds 131-155 mph (114-135 kt). More extensive wall failure. Some complete roof structure failure on small homes. Major erosion of beach areas. Land may flood very far inland.
- **Category 5 Hurricane**. Winds 156 mph and up (135+ kt). Many complete roof failures. Some complete buildings fail. Small utility buildings blown over or away. Major flood damage to lower floors. All structures near shoreline affected. Massive evacuation of residential areas.

From the Saffir-Simpson Hurricane Scale, www.nhc.noaa.gov/HAW2/english/basics/saffir_simpson.shtml

Answer It

Answer each question in one or more complete sentences.

1. Contrast a hurricane with an ordinary storm, using a T-chart.
2. Categorize these storms by types:
   a. a storm with winds of 40 mph
   b. a storm with winds of 75 mph
   c. a storm with winds of 60 mph
   d. a storm with winds of 100 mph
3. Describe how a hurricane dies out.
4. Use a Venn diagram to compare and contrast a Category 1 and Category 2 hurricane. Use information from the chart on page 49.
5. What can you conclude about a Category 5 hurricane?

Exercise 1 • Check for Understanding: Lessons 11–15

- Read the selection and follow the directions below.
- Use the Handbook section of the *Student Text* as needed.

from "Tornadoes"

What exactly is a tornado? It is a violently rotating column of air. A tornado has two important characteristics. First of all, most tornadoes form over land. In the U.S., most tornadoes develop in the center of the country between Texas and Minnesota. Tornadoes also take shape over land in other parts of the world too. Second, the swirling winds of a tornado must reach from the clouds to the ground. Most tornadoes travel about one to four miles along the ground. On average, the tip of a tornado on the ground is about 75 yards across. But some tornadoes are more than a mile wide! A tornado is one of nature's most powerful forces.

1. Find five multisyllable words. Write the words here.

____

____

2. Listen to your teacher dictate sentences for you to write. Check each sentence for correct use of capitals and end punctuation. Also check for the correct use of the **Doubling** and **Drop e** rules.

____

____

____

____

(continued)

Exercise 1 • Check for Understanding: Lessons 11 - 15 *(continued)*

____

____

____

____

3. Use one of the **Use the Clues** strategies to define the word "tornado" in "Tornadoes!" Write the meaning of the word? What strategy did you use?

4. ____

____

____

____

____

5. Create an **Informal (Two-Column) Outline** to show the topic, supporting details, and E's for the passage in the box

Topic: Characteristics of a Tornado

☆	
☆	

Bridge Resources

Consonant Chart

Type of Consonant Sound		Mouth Position						
		Lips	Lips/Teeth	Tongue Between Teeth	Tongue Behind Teeth	Roof of Mouth	Back of Mouth	Throat
	Stops	/ b / / p /			/ t / / d /		/ k / / g /	
	Fricatives		/ f / / v /	/ th / / th /	/ s / / z /	/ sh /		/ h /
	Affricatives					/ j / / ch /		
	Nasals	/ m /			/ n /		/ ng /	
	Lateral				/ l /			
	Semivowels	/ w / / hw /			/ r /	/ y /		

Vowel Chart

ē

1. ________
2. ________
3. ________
4. ________
5. ________
6. ________
7. ________
8. ________

ĭ

1. ________
2. ________
3. ________

ā

1. ________
2. ________
3. ________
4. ________
5. ________
6. ________
7. ________
8. ________
9. ________

ĕ

1. ________
2. ________

ă

1. ________

ī

1. ________
2. ________
3. ________
4. ________
5. ________
6. ________

1. ________
2. ________
3. ________
4. ________
5. ________

ŏ

1. ________
2. ________
3. ________

ŭ

1. ________
2. ________
3. ________
4. ________
5. ________

aw

1. ________
2. ________
3. ________
4. ________
5. ________
6. ________

ō

1. ________
2. ________
3. ________
4. ________
5. ________
6. ________
7. ________

o͝o

1. ________
2. ________
3. ________
4. ________

o͞o

1. ________
2. ________
3. ________
4. ________
5. ________
6. ________
7. ________
8. ________

Bridge

Essential Words (Book A) Personal Status Checklist

▸ Put a check mark (✓) in the box next to the words you misspelled on the pretest.

Essential Words	Trials		
	1	2	3
❑ are			
❑ I			
❑ is			
❑ that			
❑ the			
❑ this			
❑ do			
❑ said			
❑ to			
❑ who			
❑ you			
❑ your			
❑ from			
❑ of			
❑ they			
❑ was			
❑ were			
❑ what			
❑ be			
❑ does			
❑ he			
❑ she			
❑ we			
❑ when			
❑ here			
❑ there			
❑ these			
❑ those			
❑ where			
❑ why			
❑ down			
❑ for			
❑ her			
❑ how			
❑ me			
❑ now			

Essential Words (Book B) Personal Status Checklist

▸ Put a check mark (✓) in the box next to the words you misspelled on the pretest.

Essential Words	Trials		
	1	2	3
❑ all			
❑ call			
❑ into			
❑ our			
❑ small			
❑ their			
❑ about			
❑ any			
❑ many			
❑ out			
❑ word			
❑ write			
❑ been			
❑ could			
❑ should			
❑ too			
❑ two			
❑ would			
❑ almost			
❑ alone			
❑ already			
❑ also			
❑ although			
❑ always			
❑ body			
❑ each			
❑ every			
❑ know			
❑ thought			
❑ very			
❑ Dr.			
❑ Mr.			
❑ Mrs.			
❑ Ms.			
❑ find			
❑ only			

Sources

Hurricane!

Blohm, Craig E. 1986. "Nature's Violent Side," adapted from *Cobblestone* (April 1986) "Natural Disasters" © 1986 Carus Publishing Company, 315 Fifth Street, Peru, IL 61354. All rights reserved. Reprinted with permission.

Dineen, Jacqueline. 2002. *Natural Disasters: Hurricanes and Typhoons*. London: Aladdin Books Ltd.

NOAA: National Weather Service. 2002. "Saffir-Simpson Hurricane Scale," from *Hurricane Awareness*. http://www.nhc.noaa.gov/HAW2/english/basics/saffir_simpson.shtml.

Wood, Jenny. 1990. *Storms: Facts, Stories, Activities*. Copyright 1990 by Two-Can Publishing Ltd., an imprint of Cooper Square Publishing. Reprinted by permission of Cooper Square Publishing.

Making Hero Sandwiches

Webster's New Thesaurus. 1995. Promotional Sales Books, Inc.

New Old Insects

Platt, Gary. 1998. "What Is Amber?" http://www.gplatt.demon.co.uk/whatis.htm.

Trivedi, Bijal P. 2002. "New Insect Order Found in Southern Africa," from *National Geographic Today* (March 28). http://news.nationalgeographic.com/news/2002/03/0328_0328_TVstickinsect.html.

Telling Time

Cummings and Lucas. 2003. "Clock a History." http://www.ernie.cummings.net/clock.htm (accessed November 2003).

University of Wisconsin Board of Regents. 1998. "It's About Time" timeline. The Why Files. http://whyfiles.org/078time/3.txt (accessed November 2003).

Time Zones

Greenwich Mean Time Homepage, http://wwp.greenwichmeantime.com/home.htm (accessed October 28, 2003).

Llewellyn, Claire, A. Phillips, and L. Norton. 1995. "Clock," from *Scholastic First Encyclopedia: How Things Work*. New York: Scholastic Publications Ltd.

Photo and Illustration Credits

Photos
21: Sopris West employee watch.
50: © 1999–2003 Getty Images, Inc.

Illustrations
16: © Picturequest, LLC.
20: © Digital Vision Ltd.
47: © 1999–2003 Getty Images, Inc.
48: © North Wind Picture Archives.